I0476744

The YouTube Manifesto

A Collection Of The Top 5 Channels For Every Category Under The Sun
Volume 1

Introduction

Youtube channels and their owners are the new generation of teachers, advisers and coaches of the modern world today. Their reach is as wide as the range of the Internet. While the depth of their videos or the expertise of their opinions may be at best debatable, no one can deny their influence.

The sheer numbers that their channel's statistics represent can rival that of traditional institutions on education, learning and other mass media. The information that can be gained from these channels is not only from the videos and the channels themselves but also from the trends of the profiles of the hosts and owners.

Young or old, amateur or expert, mainstream or subculture, popular or niche, not one demographic or genre has a monopoly on success on Youtube. Virtually anybody can upload a video, create a channel and become a host or a speaker.

To help you navigate your way into the millions of channels found in Youtube and find and choose the best channels that you can subscribe to, this book will show you the top 5 channels and their statistics. It will make use of the Manifesto Rating System to help you judge them on your own preferences and opinions.

The Categories in Volume 1 of the Youtube Manifesto are:

1. DIY & How To's
2. Cooking
3. Video Games
4. Cars & Automobiles
5. Fitness & Workouts Routines for Men & Women

6. Fashion, Accessories & Lifestyle for Men & Women
7. Makeup Tutorials
8. Parenting Advice & Stories
9. Dating & Relationships
10. Motivation & Inspiration

The Categories in Volume 2 are:

1. Kindle Publishing
2. eBay Selling
3. Amazon FBA
4. Craigslist Selling
5. ETSY Selling
6. Gadgets
7. Pet Care
8. Language Learning
9. Art, Drawing, Painting & Etc
10. Computer Programming

Begin your search for the best channels today!

♥ **Copyright 2014 by Michelle Davenport- All rights reserved.**

This document is geared towards providing exact and reliable information in regards to the topic and issue covered. The publication is sold with the idea that the publisher is not required to render accounting, officially permitted, or otherwise, qualified services. If advice is necessary, legal or professional, a practiced individual in the profession should be ordered.

- From a Declaration of Principles which was accepted and approved equally by a Committee of the American Bar Association and a Committee of Publishers and Associations.

In no way is it legal to reproduce, duplicate, or transmit any part of this document in either electronic means or in printed format. Recording of this publication is strictly prohibited and any storage of this document is not allowed unless with written permission from the publisher. All rights reserved.

The information provided herein is stated to be truthful and consistent, in that any liability, in terms of inattention or otherwise, by any usage or abuse of any policies, processes, or directions contained within is the solitary and utter responsibility of the recipient reader. Under no circumstances will any legal responsibility or blame be held against the publisher for any reparation, damages, or monetary loss due to the information herein, either directly or indirectly.

Respective authors own all copyrights not held by the publisher.

The information herein is offered for informational purposes solely, and is universal as so. The presentation of the information is without contract or any type of guarantee assurance.

The trademarks that are used are without any consent, and the publication of the trademark is without permission or backing by the trademark owner. All trademarks and brands within this book are for clarifying purposes only and are the owned by the owners themselves, not affiliated with this document.

Table of Contents

Chapter One: The Youtube Manifesto

The Youtube & Channel Phenomenon

If a picture can paint a thousand words, then a video clip can certainly paint more. This is the reason why Youtube has exploded into mainstream culture, overtaking traditional media for communication. While video clips are certainly too numerous to count, there is an equally large quantity of video owners who transformed their videos into something much more.

Youtube channels represent a collection of videos that is focused on a specific content, topic or genre. The ease and accessibility of being part of the Youtube platform has created a new breed of Internet citizen, channel owners. They give advice; provide instructions, offer opinions, share reviews and other activities that once were only done through text and the written message. Youtube is now filled to the brim with these modern information providers.

The benefits of these channels are two way, both for the viewers and the owners. The viewers can have access to free source of information. For the owners, a successful channel can be a lucrative business. They can host sponsors and advertisements, which pay them a fee. Anything from featuring their product or to even just mentioning it, can be convertible to cash. While the flow of information is certainly a welcome phenomenon, there is also danger in these sources of information.

Whether the channel is truly an expert in the subject matter or only a casual or novice commentator, the owner can upload anytime and anywhere whatever information he wants. To resolve these issues on credibility, Youtube compiles certain statistics that may provide evidence on the channel's legitimacy.

Some of the statistics that Youtube keeps track of are:

1. Number of views

2. Number of subscribers

3. Number of likes and dislikes

4. Number of videos uploaded and time of uploading

The idea is, the more views and subscribers a channel has, the greater is its reach. The more likes a video clip has, the more positive is the feedback from the viewers. The more videos are uploaded, the more in depth and wider the range of the content is.

The Manifesto Rating System

To help you navigate your way to the potentially millions of videos and channels, the Manifesto Rating System is developed. Although the number of views and subscribers are certainly good indicators for a channel's credibility and potential, the System goes further to include other non-quantitative measurements. Furthermore, the System assigns weight to every criterion that makes up the final verdict on the channel. For example, the System gives a greater weight to the quality of the content of videos uploaded compared to intervals of uploads. This System emphasizes quality over quantity.

Here is the Rating System:

Content Progression & Value of Information over Time
20%

Number of Videos Uploaded
20%

Clarity of the Speaker's Voice and Content Being Delivered
15%

Likes vs. Dislikes Ratio
15%

Number of Views
  10%

Number of Subscribers
  10%

Frequency of Uploads
  10%

Total
  100%

Final Verdict

A   91-100%

B   81-90%

C   71-80%

D   Below 70%

Take note that the statistics will definitely have changed after the release of this book. The Likes vs. Dislikes ratio is generated from the most popular video in the channel. The frequency of the uploaded videos is approximations based on the timestamps on the most recent videos uploaded. Value of information is defined as the uniqueness and utility of the video content, such as a fresh take or an innovation on a common sense idea. Clarity of the voice takes into account not only the literal voice of the host but also the demeanor, personality and approachability.

As you can see, the Manifesto does not rely on numbers or statistics alone. The Top 5 channels you will see on the list may not have the greatest number of videos or the millions of subscribers. Some of the channels are on the Top 5 because they offer a different take on the category they belong to or because they are relatively new but offer great potential.

For example, in the Motivational Category, there is a channel that only has less than 20 videos but the number of views and the quality of each video make it truly a gem in the category.

There are other notable peculiarities in the Channel Industry:

1. You may expect that the Youtube accounts of the institutions and well-known brands will have the greatest number of views and subscribers but it is always not the case. In fact, the lone girl barely out of her teenage years is the one that commands a greater following. The lesson here is that amateur channel owners can play with the established brands out there in the leveled playing field of Youtube. This shows that when you choose channels to subscribe to, you may also want to consider channels owned by individuals or small groups.

2. Big and costly productions have more or less the same statistics as the frugal channel owner. The lesson here is that a channel does not have to cost much to become successful but the host must make up for the gap in the production. You may want to give a second chance to channels that seem to be low budget, they may have the information and content that you need.

3. In a world where diversity, not uniformity, is celebrated, the Manifesto takes into account this trend. Included in the Top 5 are not only your typical and mainstream channels but also the owners who represent other opinions, style and information in the category. The lesson here is that focused and niche channels can compete with mainstream counterparts. When you are surfing Youtube channels, be sure to keep your mind open for other sources not only the established but also the new and progressive.

The Categories

The Categories in Volume 1 are:

11. DIY & How To's
12. Cooking
13. Video Games
14. Cars & Automobiles
15. Fitness & Workouts Routines for Men & Women
16. Fashion, Accessories & Lifestyle for Men & Women
17. Makeup Tutorials
18. Parenting Advice & Stories
19. Dating & Relationships
20. Motivation & Inspiration

Each Category has the Top 5 Channels based on the Manifesto's rating, except for the men and women-specific categories that have their own 5 channels.

The template for the information for each channel is:

Channel Name: This is the name or title of the channel. You may use the words here to search for the channel in Youtube.

Link: This a clickable link that will bring you directly to the Home page of the channel.

Rank: This has the number 5 to 1, 5 being the lowest and 1 being the highest.

Description: This is a brief summary of the channel; it may include information provided by the channel owner or through a brief rundown of the videos in the channel.

Statistics:
Total View Count: This is the number of views
Video Uploaded: This is the number of videos uploaded
Number of Subscribers: This is the number of subscribers

Average Likes vs. Dislike Ratio: This is number of likes and dislikes found on the most popular video of the channel. The number of votes is added and then the numbers of likes are given a percentage

Average Frequency of Uploads: This is the approximate timeframe when a new video is uploaded.

Comments:

Content Progression & Value of Information
This is a description of the development and the value of the content given in the channel.

Clarity of the Speaker's Voice and Content
This is a description of the way the host presents himself, both through verbal and non-verbal means of communication.

Verdict: This is a letter from A to D that represents the final rating for the channel as a whole and not a specific video in the channel. A brief explanation for the rating is also included.

Chapter Two: DIY & How To's

Channel Name: Laur DIY

Link: https://www.youtube.com/user/LaurDIY

Rank: 5

Description:

A young host that offers DIY projects from room decorations, holiday gift ideas to workouts, and this channel helps viewers satisfy organizing, healthy and home decorating needs.

Statistics:

Total View Count: 68,729,531
Video Uploaded: 247
Number of Subscribers: 1,499,997
Average Likes vs. Dislike Ratio: 41,294 vs. 331 /99% Liked
Average Frequency of Uploads: Once a week

Comments:

Content Progression & Value of Information
The content is geared towards the host's demographics, young, female and passionate for life. Videos are well organized in the playlist tab.

Clarity of the Speaker's Voice and Content
The host is energetic and full of life; her personality makes the viewers engaged in not only watching but also applying the lessons in the video.

Verdict: C

It is a great channel and extremely fun and informative. You will not get bored watching each of the videos as they offer creativity and novelty to new projects.

Channel Name: Ask the Builder

Link: https://www.youtube.com/user/AsktheBuilder

Rank: 4

Description:

For your home improvement and maintenance needs, this channel offers the advice of an expert host in everything house related.

Statistics:

Total View Count: 38,489,342
Video Uploaded: 475
Number of Subscribers: 49,806
Average Likes vs. Dislike Ratio: 1,102 vs. 105 / 91% Liked
Average Frequency of Uploads: Once to twice a month

Comments:

Content Progression & Value of Information
There is a wide variety of repairs and improvement videos. Tools, equipments and tricks are also shared. The weather-specific content is also valuable.

Clarity of the Speaker's Voice and Content
The host's overall look and personality give credibility to his craft. He is not only well-informed but also lives the videos he makes. Every viewer will feel confident watching his videos.

Verdict: B

A perfect channel for your simple to major home improvement needs that you want to do on your own.

Channel Name: Lifehacker

Link: https://www.youtube.com/user/lifehacker

Rank: 3

Description:

This channel covers almost everything under the sun with its tips, tricks and shortcuts. The hosts offers more than just function but also fun and entertainment.

Statistics:

Total View Count: 40,392,582
Video Uploaded: 788
Number of Subscribers: 205,554
Average Likes vs. Dislike Ratio: 4,076 vs., 2,838 / 59% Liked
Average Frequency of Uploads: Once a month

Comments:

Content Progression & Value of Information
The value of this channel is in its diversity of videos. It does not stop with function but even the impractical but funny hacks for everyone.

Clarity of the Speaker's Voice and Content
The strengths of this channel are not only the actual lifehacks but also the hosts. They are a group of guys and a gal who throw banter, along with their tips and tricks.

Verdict: B

You will most probably find this channel when you are looking for a specific solution. Once you find it, you will be hooked into watching the other videos. The ratio may be an isolated case as other videos are positively received.

Channel Name: Martha Stewart

Link: https://www.youtube.com/user/MarthaStewart

Rank: 2

Description:

The queen of all DIY crafts, recipes and lifestyle, this is the channel for the classic DIY aficionado.

Statistics:
Total View Count: 23,860,360
Video Uploaded: 1,538
Number of Subscribers: 117,151
Average Likes vs. Dislike Ratio: 4,243 vs. 98 / 98% Liked
Average Frequency of Uploads: Once to twice a week

Comments:
Content Progression & Value of Information
There is no contest to the value of the information given by the host. It covers a wide range of tips for everything related to your home and more.

Clarity of the Speaker's Voice and Content
The authority of the host cannot be disputed, she alone gives credibility to the videos in the channel. Her guests give an added dimension to the channel.

Verdict: B

Although there is no contest to the reputation and expertise of the host and the channel, they may be considered old-fashioned in a modern world. Certainly, there are other channels in the market that offer a fresher take on similar problems.

Channel Name: Howcast

Link: https://www.youtube.com/user/Howcast

Rank: 1

Description:

A DIY and How-to channel, it is one of the most prolific in Youtube, with thousands of videos. It covers almost anything under the sun for both men and women.

Statistics:

Total View Count: 1,729,012,144
Video Uploaded: 21,850
Number of Subscribers: 3,054,293
Average Likes vs. Dislike Ratio: 34,747 vs. 14,415 / 71% Liked
Average Frequency of Uploads: Once to twice a week

Comments:
Content Progression & Value of Information
Another channel that draws strength from its diversity of videos, it offers unique advice that can be well-received by viewers from all demographics.

Clarity of the Speaker's Voice and Content
Instead of only one host, the channel features several experts for the specific objective of each video. This makes the channel very well-rounded and at the same time credible.

Verdict: A

This is the channel that combines the best of all worlds, diversity mixed with expertise and energized by fresh ideas.

Chapter Three: Cooking

Channel Name: Laura in the Kitchen

Link:
https://www.youtube.com/user/LauraVitalesKitchen/featured

Rank: 5

Description:

This channel presents a variety of Italian recipes. It is hosted by Laura Vitale, who was born and raised in Italy. She moved to the US at the age of 12 and helped her father open several restaurants. The businesses closed after the economic downturn. She continues her father's legacy and her heritage of cooking good food through sharing the recipes with her subscribers. The channel is part of a network of social media, including Facebook, Twitter, Instagram, a dedicated blog and website.

Statistics:

Total View Count: 220,420,466
Video Uploaded: 1,456
Number of Subscribers: 1,864,271
Average Likes vs. Dislike Ratio: 22,032 vs. 1,063 / 96% Liked
Average Frequency of Uploads: Once every 2 days

Comments:

Content Progression & Value of Information
Videos are informative and timely. Recipes are paired with the season or holiday when the video was made. Great variety of recipes, the usual pasta recipes are there but there is so much more. There are desserts, pastries, vegan, protein and other recipes that can be appreciated by any viewer. Most of the recipes are easy to prepare and does not require complicated kitchen knowledge to execute.

Clarity of the Speaker's Voice and Content
Laura, the host and owner of the channel, is very lively, animated and unapologetically Italian. A slightly fast talker, probably to highlight the quickness of the preparation of the recipes she is cooking. She is a very professional cooking show host, she makes sure to describe every step in detail.

Verdict: B

It is a perfect channel for those in search of authentic Italian recipes that go beyond the typical pasta recipes. Although the host talks fast, the captions make up for it. There are no product endorsements that give the channel an unbiased presentation of the best ingredients for the recipes.
Channel Name: Jamie Oliver's Food

Link: https://www.youtube.com/user/JamieOliver

Rank: 4

Description:

This channel is top billed by Jamie Oliver but he is only one of the many cooks that take part in this foodie channel. Several cooks, each with their own take in food and life take turns hosting the videos. It highlights the importance of fresh talent with a dash of comic relief and guaranteed delicious recipes.

Statistics:

Total View Count: 101,440,556
Video Uploaded: 1,899
Number of Subscribers: 1,481,904
Average Likes vs. Dislike Ratio: 5,704 vs. 2,032 / 73% Liked
Average Frequency of Uploads: Once a day

Comments:

Content Progression & Value of Information
The channel hosts are straightforward; they go right to the cooking instructions and complement it with good visuals. Camera angles are good; it gives you a perfect view of the food being cooked instead of focusing on the chef alone.

Clarity of the Speaker's Voice and Content
Jamie Oliver and his community of cooks and chefs represent a diverse set of personality. Each of them has their own voice, style and unique take on cooking. This makes the content not only rich and informative but also avoids monotony and repetition.

Verdict: B

Watching this channel gives you access to the expertise of not only one cook. The variety and the organization of the videos, from short and quick recipes to 20 minutes videos, make it a nice source of a variety of information. This channel is recommended for those in search of videos for cooking beginners.

Channel Name: Cooking with Dog

Link: https://www.youtube.com/user/cookingwithdog

Rank: 3

Description:

A mystery chef narrates the step by step guide for the mainly Japanese recipes, while a Japanese lady does the cooking. Aside from the recipes, the main highlight is Francis, a gray poodle that sits on the countertop watching the cooking of the recipes. The dog gives the unexpected twist in a cooking show, providing some comic relief with his various reactions.

Statistics:

Total View Count: 114,115,150
Video Uploaded: 228
Number of Subscribers: 957,306
Average Likes vs. Dislike Ratio: 48,883 vs. 716 / 99% Liked
Average Frequency of Uploads: Once a week

Comments:

Content Progression & Value of Information
Focusing mainly on Japanese dishes such as sushi, rice bowls and ramen, viewers will appreciate the expertise provided by the channel.

Clarity of the Speaker's Voice and Content
The mystery narrator speaks English but has a thick Japanese accent that may make it difficult for viewers to understand. Given time, viewers will get used to it.

Verdict: C

A unique channel that may cater to a specific niche of viewers, this channel does not fail to provide delicious Japanese recipes and dishes. The monotony of the narrator can almost be ignored because of the canine host that looks on to the Japanese cook. If you like dogs and Japanese food, this channel will be perfect for you.

Channel Name: Lean Body Lifestyle

Link:
https://www.youtube.com/channel/UCb9ageBPhZYNBU93tn
js-QA

Rank: 2

Description:

For the body builders, a low-fat and protein aficionado, this
channel is hosted by Michael Kory and his physique gives
credibility to the effectiveness of his recipes.

Statistics:

Total View Count: 14,969,285
Video Uploaded: 200
Number of Subscribers: 223,142
Average Likes vs. Dislike Ratio: 11,661 vs. 57 / 99% Liked
Average Frequency of Uploads: Once a week

Comments:

Content Progression & Value of Information
The diversity of the videos makes it a total lifestyle channel for
body builders, who want a channel that gives information on
fitness, recipes and workouts. Recipes videos are uploaded
side by side with workout for abs, biceps, chests and other
body parts.

Clarity of the Speaker's Voice and Content
Aside from the recipes, the host provides tidbits of information
that adds to the lifestyle of a lean body builder.

Verdict: B

If you are looking for the total fitness channel that covers both
diet and workout program, this is the channel to subscribe.

Channel Name: Sorted Food

Link: https://www.youtube.com/user/sortedfood

Rank: 1

Description:

This is a channel that covers a wide variety of food. Recipes from across the globe that include breakfasts, mains and desserts are included. The hosts are charismatic, relaxed and add fun to cooking.

Statistics:

Total View Count: 11,052,394
Video Uploaded: 763
Number of Subscribers: 1,141,224
Average Likes vs. Dislike Ratio: 22,989 vs. 346 / 98% Liked
Average Frequency of Uploads: Once every 2 days

Comments:

Content Progression & Value of Information
The primary advantage of this channel is the diversity. It goes beyond recipes; the hosts regularly invite guest chefs and cooks to add variety to their already growing number of videos.

Clarity of the Speaker's Voice and Content
The three hosts make for an engaging video. Their playful banter gives a welcome addition to the cooking show. The channel is very accommodating to their viewers, featuring requests for recipes. It gives a youthful and fresh look to an industry dominated by experienced cooks.

Verdict: A

A channel that gives a relaxed take to the serious task of cooking, the hosts are able to add fun to make even the hesitant amateur cook feel motivated to try the recipes. This is where the value of this channel can be found, its ability to engage and inspire action.

Chapter Four: Video Games

Channel Name: Markiplier

Link: https://www.youtube.com/user/markiplierGAME

Rank: 5

Description:

A horror game aficionado, the host is able to add comedy to an otherwise scary video game genre. The channel combines comedy and parodies with the gamer are lifestyle. The videos are not only entertaining but also informative.

Statistics:

Total View Count: 2,008,335,195
Video Uploaded: 2,238
Number of Subscribers: 7,045,546
Average Likes vs. Dislike Ratio: 239,227 vs. 13,702 / 95% Liked
Average Frequency of Uploads: Once to twice a day

Comments:

Content Progression & Value of Information
The game videos are interspersed with other videos that are more about the host's life, personal situations and other topics. Although this may be acceptable to some, it may also make it hard for viewers to navigate through the entire channel.

Clarity of the Speaker's Voice and Content
Engaging with a bit of drama, the host gives clear instructions on how to navigate and win through each of the various games' levels covered in the channel.

Verdict: C

While the game contents are very useful, other videos mixed in
the list may discourage viewers to see it as a serious video
game channel.

Channel Name: Let's Play

Link: https://www.youtube.com/user/LetsPlay

Rank: 4

Description:

The channel is all about the gaming life of a group of friends. Video clips of the actual games and the reactions of the gamers make this channel both informative and fun to watch.

Statistics:

Total View Count: 845,822,552
Video Uploaded: 844
Number of Subscribers: 3,224,967
Average Likes vs. Dislike Ratio: 63,231 vs. 1,725 / 97% Liked
Average Frequency of Uploads: Once to twice a day

Comments:

Content Progression & Value of Information
The videos are able to cover the entire play through of the games that are being featured. For a gamer, this level of completeness will be invaluable.

Clarity of the Speaker's Voice and Content
It may be easy to get lost in the banter between the hosts while covering the games they feature. However, this level of trash talking may make a hardcore gamer feel right at home.

Verdict: B

This is the authentic gaming channel experience, made and hosted by gamers for gamers.

Channel Name: Hutch

Link: https://www.youtube.com/user/shaun0728

Rank: 3

Description:

This is a channel that specializes in the first person shooter genre of video games. The videos present replays for strategies for action packed engagements

Statistics:

Total View Count: 111,583,668
Video Uploaded: 778
Number of Subscribers: 876,993
Average Likes vs. Dislike Ratio: 34,584 vs. 449 / 99% Liked
Average Frequency of Uploads: Once a day

Comments:

Content Progression & Value of Information
Game play and rules of engagement are the selling points of this channel. These two are absolute necessity for the competitive game play of the shooter genre.

Clarity of the Speaker's Voice and Content
The host is fully immersed in the game, complete with emotions, instructions and the occasional profanity.

Verdict: B

If you have the same preference for shooter games, then this channel will be heaven for you. The videos are crisp making you feel as though you are playing the games yourself.

Channel Name: Game Grumps

Link: https://www.youtube.com/user/GameGrumps

Rank: 2

Description:

A laid back and nostalgic channel but without the boredom and monotony of casual gamers, this channel features a combination of classic games in old consoles to the latest games.

Statistics:

Total View Count: 1,034,737,824
Video Uploaded: 2,640
Number of Subscribers: 2,195,444
Average Likes vs. Dislike Ratio: 39,443 vs. 777 / 98% Liked
Average Frequency of Uploads: Once a day

Comments:

Content Progression & Value of Information
An eclectic mix of old and new games, the channel shows the game play for some of the earliest video games.

Clarity of the Speaker's Voice and Content
The hosts lend their own voices to the animated cartoons that represent them. They add personality in the commentary of their featured games.

Verdict: B

This is a breath of fresh air in the channel category. While most channels focus on the latest games in the market, the hosts play the classic games. It is a welcome respite from the high tech videos in the category.

Channel Name: Machinima

Link: https://www.youtube.com/user/machinima

Rank: 1

Description:

This channel features almost all new games in the market. It includes teaser trailers, game plays, tips and reviews.

Statistics:

Total View Count: 5,326,474,301
Video Uploaded: 25,115
Number of Subscribers: 12,363,728
Average Likes vs. Dislike Ratio: 48,142 vs. 11,901 / 80% Liked
Average Frequency of Uploads: Once a day

Comments:

Content Progression & Value of Information
The sheer numbers of the videos uploaded give this channel the diversity that no other channel in the category may be capable of amassing.

Clarity of the Speaker's Voice and Content
Virtual institutions in the genre, the two hosts are respected for their love and passion for the game. Aside from providing information themselves, they also invite guests to the channel. The guests are the insiders of the games they feature, such as developers and creative design team members.

Verdict: A

Machinima is on a league of its own in the Gaming channels of Youtube. It is the absolute go to for the latest games from a variety of genres. From the first time to the avid gamer, this channel will be very popular.

Chapter Five: Cars & Automobiles

Channel Name: Autocar

Link: https://www.youtube.com/user/autocar

Rank: 5

Description:

This channel has a pool of experts that delivers car reviews and showcases some of the world's fastest, most exotic and exciting cars. Aside from the automobiles, this channel also shows race tracks and roads.

 Statistics:

Total View Count: 191,057,071
Video Uploaded: 784
Number of Subscribers: 461,293
Average Likes vs. Dislike Ratio: 8,680 vs. 1,616 / 84% Liked
Average Frequency of Uploads: Once a week

Comments:

Content Progression & Value of Information
This channel is able to provide a front seat experience to the viewers on their featured cars. They bring you right into the action and provide expert advice and opinions.

Clarity of the Speaker's Voice and Content
The host covers every detail of the car that is featured. From the driving, to the accessories to the handling of the car, the host discusses them in equally.

Verdict: C

This channel is able to provide a detailed review of the car they feature; their commentaries match the target customers of the car. This makes this channel extremely informative to the viewers in search for information on a specific car. The only downside is that it might not have the adventure and excitement that are often sought after by car aficionados.

Channel Name: Jay Leno's Garage

Link: https://www.youtube.com/user/JayLenosGarage

Rank: 4

Description:

Jay Leno himself shows off his collection of cars plus conducts reviews for cars, motorcycles and other automobiles. Aside from luxury cars, he also shows vintage, racers and other super cars.

Statistics:

Total View Count: 137,419,481
Video Uploaded: 410
Number of Subscribers: 1,256,764
Average Likes vs. Dislike Ratio: 25,372 vs. 865 / 97% Liked
Average Frequency of Uploads: Once a week

Comments:

Content Progression & Value of Information
Aside from being hosted by an expert and a collector, the value of this channel is taken from the diverse cars that are featured. Only few channels have this focus on both vintage and modern cars, motorcycles and other car accessories.

Clarity of the Speaker's Voice and Content
Credibility is the main strength of this channel, the host is able to provide this authority with his expert insight and the guests he invites in the videos.

Verdict: A

One of America's well-known car collectors, the host is able to speak from experience in reviewing the cars featured. As the owner of most of the cars in the channel, he is able to speak the car aficionado language.

Channel Name: Everyday Driver

Link: https://www.youtube.com/user/EverydayDriver

Rank: 3

Description:

One of the most popular and youngest channels, the channel is gaining popularity across the world by providing a new take on the industry. It provides crisp images to both the average and car obsessed viewers.

Statistics:

Total View Count: 18,645,529
Video Uploaded: 136
Number of Subscribers: 91,241
Average Likes vs. Dislike Ratio: 4,862 vs. 197 / 96% Liked
Average Frequency of Uploads: Once a week

Comments:

Content Progression & Value of Information
The channel divides reviews and features of one car into several videos; this makes each video focused and organized on specific areas. At the same time, it is able to progress and link the next video with the previous one.

Clarity of the Speaker's Voice and Content
While the focus of the channel is on providing images and various camera angles for every car featured, the host is still able to provide reviews and information. This technique allows a bird's eye view for the featured cars.

Verdict: B

The fly-by, interior and driver's seat point of view camera angles give this channel a fresh take on the genre.

Channel Name: Top Gear

Link: https://www.youtube.com/user/TopGear

Rank: 2

Description:

One of the most comprehensive channels, it covers a wide variety of cars of all shapes and sizes. It travels around the world to showcase some of the most expensive, cheapest and average priced cars.

Statistics:

Total View Count: 943,229,280
Video Uploaded: 843
Number of Subscribers: 4,362,056
Average Likes vs. Dislike Ratio: 64,091 vs. 2,802 / 96% Liked
Average Frequency of Uploads: Once a week

Comments:

Content Progression & Value of Information
This channel may be the only one of its kind, in terms of the lengths it will take to provide content. Some of the information and scenes given in the videos may not be done anywhere else.

Clarity of the Speaker's Voice and Content
The hosts mix their technical expertise with comedic episodes to make the discussion more entertaining. The experiments they make are exciting ways to drive their points across.

Verdict: A

One of the highlights of the channel is when the host pits one car to another type of vehicle, such as a motor to even a jet fighter. Other times, it even completely crashes and destroys cars. The adventure found in these videos gives the channel this rating.

Channel Name: Drive

Link: https://www.youtube.com/user/drive

Rank: 1

Description:

Instead of featuring only cars, this channel brings viewers to the races, roads, factories and the studio where the car can be found.

Statistics:

Total View Count: 241,676,911
Video Uploaded: 993
Number of Subscribers: 1,335,716
Average Likes vs. Dislike Ratio: 24,307 vs. 960 / 96% Liked
Average Frequency of Uploads: Once a day

Comments:

Content Progression & Value of Information
This channel goes beyond the cars they feature, they break the cars into its essential parts, from the car seats, the wheels to the paint and even to the studios that showcase them. It gives the total car lifestyle experience to the viewer.

Clarity of the Speaker's Voice and Content
The host invites guests and other speakers to add weight, quantity and credibility to the various insights and opinions given in the channel.

Verdict: A

Going beyond statistics and with style that is out of the box for traditional car channels, this channel's ability to give viewers access to this wealth of information, insight and imagery make it one of the absolute must subscribe for car enthusiasts.

Chapter Six: Fitness & Workout Routines

For Men

Channel Name: Frugal Fitness TV

Link: https://www.youtube.com/user/MyFrugalFitness

Rank: 5

Description:

A self confessed cheapskate, the host encourages a fitness lifestyle that is not costly and can be done at the comforts of the viewer's home.

Statistics:

Total View Count: 871,626
Video Uploaded: 304
Number of Subscribers: 8,119
Average Likes vs. Dislike Ratio: 372 vs. 30 / 93% Liked
Average Frequency of Uploads: Once every 6 months

Comments:

Content Progression & Value of Information
The value of this channel is its unique take on fitness. While most channels will feature gym memberships, supplements, equipment, this channel is able to achieve the same benefits with the least expense.

Clarity of the Speaker's Voice and Content
The host demonstrates each of his ideas and speaks in a clear tone. He is not shy to mention some of his own needs for fitness, which gives the viewer some degree of confidence on his honesty.

Verdict: A

Although the statistics may be low, just by the sheer uniqueness of this channel, its focus on frugality, this channel receives the top rating.

Channel Name: Omar Isuf

Link: https://www.youtube.com/user/OmarIsuf

Rank: 4

Description:

This channel provides a variety of fitness regimens for the true bodybuilder. It features both things to do and things to avoid.

Statistics:

Total View Count: 43,719,429
Video Uploaded: 673
Number of Subscribers: 325,451
Average Likes vs. Dislike Ratio: 9,860 vs. 751 / 93% Liked
Average Frequency of Uploads: Once to twice a week

Comments:

Content Progression & Value of Information
For those who are totally into bulking up, the videos in the channel will satisfy the viewer's information needs.

Clarity of the Speaker's Voice and Content
Although the host does provide several tips on fitness, it all comes from his own experience. Since each fitness regimen must match the person's own health background, not all of the host's advice may work. The saving grace of this channel is the honesty of the host in telling the lessons from his mistakes.

Verdict: C

This channel shows both the do's and don'ts for fitness. The host has experienced the mistakes himself, so he can speak from experience. He includes workouts for all body types.

Channel Name: Six Pack Shortcuts

Link: v https://www.youtube.com/user/sixpackshortcuts

Rank: 3

Description:

This channels shows viewers how to get ripped, lose fat and gain muscle mass. The highlights are tricks that can help viewers reach their goals faster than usual.

Statistics:

Total View Count: 427,891,252
Video Uploaded: 380
Number of Subscribers: 3,240,855
Average Likes vs. Dislike Ratio: 97,983 vs. 3,364/ 97% Liked
Average Frequency of Uploads: Once to twice a week

Comments:

Content Progression & Value of Information
One of the things that make this channel unique is the host's videos on information on why a fitness program may not work for you. While other channels only show the ideal versions of the workout, the host also presents common mistakes and errors so that the viewers will be able to avoid them.

Clarity of the Speaker's Voice and Content
The host is able to put himself in the shoes of his viewers. In the perfect world, every fitness program will work but in the real world, things will not always go as planned. The host gives information on the potential errors of the viewer's program.

Verdict: A

The cautionary videos make this video extremely valuable. It goes beyond the fitness programs that work, it also teaches you what may not.

Channel Name: Strength Camp

Link: https://www.youtube.com/user/strengthcamp

Rank: 2

Description:

This channel makes use of almost all gym equipment available for the total body workout. There are videos that show viewers how to engage all the muscle groups.

Statistics:

Total View Count: 194,627,298
Video Uploaded: 1,261
Number of Subscribers: 1,273,008
Average Likes vs. Dislike Ratio: 30,597 vs. 958/ 97% Liked
Average Frequency of Uploads: Once to twice a month

Comments:

Content Progression & Value of Information
The information provided in this channel goes beyond fitness; it also shows the viewers problem areas in their workout that need to be avoided. Also it shows the other benefits of fitness aside from physical advantages.

Clarity of the Speaker's Voice and Content
The passion and the drive of the host are very motivating. He speaks with confidence and has technical expertise on the topics he discusses.

Verdict: B

This is a true body building channel for those in search for the bigger frames and bulkier muscles. Although the exercises may only be applicable to specific body type, the information is perfect for those who share the host's body type.

Channel Name: Scott Herman Fitness

Link: https://www.youtube.com/user/ScottHermanFitness

Rank: 1

Description:

This channel aims to provide a new routine and exercise every week. It only shares videos that are proven, such as fat loss, muscle gain and endurance training.

Statistics:

Total View Count: 139,273,317
Video Uploaded: 1,088
Number of Subscribers: 719,480
Average Likes vs. Dislike Ratio: 15,327 vs. 1,026 / 94% Liked
Average Frequency of Uploads: Once to twice a week

Comments:

Content Progression & Value of Information
It is one of the most prolific channels in the category. It goes to great lengths to provide the total workout experience for all muscle groups using a variety of gym equipment.

Clarity of the Speaker's Voice and Content
One of the strengths of the host is his openness to listening to his viewers and fans. He uses this feedback as the basis for his new videos.

Verdict: A

The host makes his own tweaks to traditional workouts. It gives a breath of fresh air from the usual way of doing the exercises.

For Women

Channel Name: Tara Stiles

Link: https://www.youtube.com/user/TaraStilesYoga

Rank: 5

Description:

This is a yoga channel for ladies that encourage viewers to try the workout without the esoteric claims.

Statistics:

Total View Count: 23,538,693
Video Uploaded: 527
Number of Subscribers: 227,404
Average Likes vs. Dislike Ratio: 9,885 vs. 328 / 97% Liked
Average Frequency of Uploads: Once a month

Comments:

Content Progression & Value of Information
Aside from the yoga videos, the channel also complements the channel with a variety of recipes that can augment the yoga lifestyle.

Clarity of the Speaker's Voice and Content
The host combines music with her narration to create a video that is more than informational. The result is a video that can be used as the actual companion video for doing yoga.

Verdict: B

The channel that includes yoga exercise for all times of the day, from morning to before bedtime, this makes the channel's information very accessible and practical to use.

Channel Name: XHIT Daily

Link: https://www.youtube.com/user/XFitDaily

Rank: 4

Description:

This channel features workouts that can be done in a daily basis. The videos provide endurance and boost the viewer's energy. The overall objective of the channel is to help readers gain the body that they want.

 Statistics:

Total View Count: 124,767,577
Video Uploaded: 608
Number of Subscribers: 1,337,840
Average Likes vs. Dislike Ratio: 94,531 vs. 1,708 / 98% Liked
Average Frequency of Uploads: Once a week

Comments:

Content Progression & Value of Information
One of the unique features of this channel is its short but effective fitness workouts that can be done for women in the go. It does not put too much focus on the use of equipment; instead it shows how exercise can be done by just using basic items that can already be available in your home.

Clarity of the Speaker's Voice and Content
The channel has a variety of hosts and guests that give their own personalities and advice to the videos.

Verdict: B

Taking inspiration from the fitness regimen that are being used by famous celebrities and models, this channel makes it highly valuable to viewers who want to achieve the look that is popular today.

Channel Name: Amanda Russell

Link: https://www.youtube.com/user/AmandaRussell

Rank: 3

Description:

This channel keeps you up to date with a wide range of topics, advice and review of fitness trends. The host also gives ideas on not only fitness but also on the total fitness lifestyle.

Statistics:

Total View Count: 5,183,084
Video Uploaded: 228
Number of Subscribers: 72,466
Average Likes vs. Dislike Ratio: 5,145 vs. 87 / 98% Liked
Average Frequency of Uploads: Once a week

Comments:
Content Progression & Value of Information
Another channel that has the same characteristics with the previous channel, the main difference is that it targets female viewers with a leaner body type.

Clarity of the Speaker's Voice and Content
Aside from the host's own body that gives credibility to her advice, she makes use of a variety of techniques aside from fitness. This shows viewers that exercise needs to be complemented with diets and other positive lifestyle choices.

Verdict: B

A perfect channel for lean female viewers, this allows viewers to have a body that has a better tone and also builds endurance.

Channel Name: BEX Life

Link: https://www.youtube.com/user/genghisgirl

Rank: 2

Description:

The host is a mom who juggles family life with her passion in fitness. She advocates not only yoga but also a lifestyle that is sustainable for your home's environment.

Statistics:

Total View Count: 21,110,700
Video Uploaded: 707
Number of Subscribers: 146,601
Average Likes vs. Dislike Ratio: 12,721 vs. 359 / 97% Liked
Average Frequency of Uploads: Once a day

Comments:

Content Progression & Value of Information
One of the most comprehensive channels in this category, it might be a fitness channel but it includes so much more information.

Clarity of the Speaker's Voice and Content
The host is able to provide credibility to the channel because of her own life experiences that reflect the diversity of her videos.

Verdict: A

This channel is more than a fitness workout; it is also a lifestyle channel for viewers who are also mothers.

Channel Name: Tone It Up

Link: https://www.youtube.com/user/ToneItUpcom

Rank: 1

Description:

A channel that was featured in a variety of women's fitness magazine around the world, this makes it one of the most recognized channels in this category.

Statistics:

Total View Count: 26,486,387
Video Uploaded: 282
Number of Subscribers: 471,775
Average Likes vs. Dislike Ratio: 8,088 vs. 131 /
Average Frequency of Uploads: Once to twice a week

Comments:

Content Progression & Value of Information
The channel takes into account the events around the viewer's year. For example, calendar dates, such as spring break, Valentine's Day and other holidays and the corresponding fitness regimen required, make this channel timely.

Clarity of the Speaker's Voice and Content
The hosts of this channel emphasize the importance of teamwork in every woman's workout. Having a friend that can support and perform the fitness exercises with you will make the sessions not only easier but also more fun.

Verdict: A

The most popular are the bikini workouts that are the best especially during the summer season. The timeliness of their fitness regimen makes this channel deserve the top spot.

Chapter Seven: Fashion, Accessories & Lifestyle

For Men

Channel Name: Art of Manliness

Link: https://www.youtube.com/user/artofmanliness

Rank: 5

Description:

A complete lifestyle guide for men, the goal of the channel is to revive the lost art of manliness.

Statistics:

Total View Count: 17,945,117
Video Uploaded: 148
Number of Subscribers: 235,440
Average Likes vs. Dislike Ratio: 1,914 vs. 145 / 93% Liked
Average Frequency of Uploads: Once a week

Comments:

Content Progression & Value of Information
The channel covers a wide variety of men's lifestyle topics, from the fashion, exercise, grooming to even cooking.

Clarity of the Speaker's Voice and Content
The host is somewhat a caricature of the stereotypical man, complete with mustache, a high sense of honor and the urge to be the top on everything.

Verdict: C

Although it is a complete lifestyle channel, some of the videos may seem outdated due to the quality and the novelty of the videos. It might not be taken seriously by the interested and modern viewer.

Channel Name: Real Men Real Style

Link: https://www.youtube.com/user/RealMenRealStyle

Rank: 4

Description:

This channel aims to provide men with the tools and education they need to create a set of clothes, wardrobes and other accessories that reflect their personality.

Statistics:

Total View Count: 17,339,716
Video Uploaded: 439
Number of Subscribers: 264,222
Average Likes vs. Dislike Ratio: 10,493 vs. 409 / 96% Liked
Average Frequency of Uploads: Once to twice a week

Comments:

Content Progression & Value of Information
This is a channel with a razor sharp focus on building a wardrobe complete with clothes, accessories and tools.

Clarity of the Speaker's Voice and Content
The host gives clear instructions, no frills no side comments. It goes straight to the point which is sure to be a desired way of communication for the male viewers.

Verdict: B

The focus of this channel gives it this rating. It does not litter its channel with unnecessary or unrelated videos.

Channel Name: Alpha M.

Link: https://www.youtube.com/user/AlphaMconsulting

Rank: 3

Description:

A channel that covers everything from style, grooming, confidence and overall image for men, the host takes also offers reviews for products. It commits to create confidence.

Statistics:

Total View Count: 43,194,117
Video Uploaded: 293
Number of Subscribers: 476,678
Average Likes vs. Dislike Ratio: 9,614 vs. 762 / 93% Liked
Average Frequency of Uploads: Once to twice a week

Comments:
Content Progression & Value of Information
The sheer courage of this channel to discuss even the most sensitive of topics makes this channel a cut above the rest. No holds barred, it is able to provide information that an average guy may hesitate to even ask but is very curious to know.

Clarity of the Speaker's Voice and Content
The confidence and bravura of the host, even touting to be anti-establishment, gives this channel and the viewer the same level of confidence in facing his own fashion fears.

Verdict: A

This is another channel that is straight to the point. It does not hesitate in giving information that puts into consideration the many types of men and their specific needs out there.

Channel Name: Jair Woo

Link: https://www.youtube.com/user/jairwoo

Rank: 2

Description:

Everything related to style are included in this channel. Reviews, lifestyle and tutorials make this hip and young channel very popular. The channel offers men's hair, DIYs, fashion and accessory advice with personal influence. The host also gives out prizes for viewers.

Statistics:

Total View Count: 17,719,301
Video Uploaded: 228
Number of Subscribers: 180,913
Average Likes vs. Dislike Ratio: 7,297 vs. 1,122 / 87% Liked
Average Frequency of Uploads: Once to twice a week

Comments:

Content Progression & Value of Information
Diversity is one of the two things that make this channel very successful. The information covers a wide range of topics that are both modern and appealing to the target demographic.

Clarity of the Speaker's Voice and Content
The other thing that makes this channel successful is the host himself. He is young and hip and able to detect and translate trends into his video tutorials.

Verdict: A

The emphasis in this channel is not to go for fashionable items but towards developing a personal style.

Channel Name: GQ

Link: https://www.youtube.com/user/GQVideos

Rank: 1

Description:

The establishment of men's fashion, this channel is the companion for the globally renowned GQ Magazine.

Statistics:

Total View Count: 57,851,671
Video Uploaded: 856
Number of Subscribers: 228,166
Average Likes vs. Dislike Ratio: 7,382 vs. 356 / 95% Liked
Average Frequency of Uploads: Once to twice a week

Comments:

Content Progression & Value of Information
The information in this channel cannot be accessed anywhere else, the guest from all walks of life and backgrounds, the commentaries and access to a vast network of experts make this channel one of a kind.

Clarity of the Speaker's Voice and Content
The variety of hosts and guests give credibility to this channel. Viewers will have confidence in the advice they receive as the information are the result of careful editing from industry experts.

Verdict: A

The institution in men's fashion, accessories and lifestyle, this is the go-to channel for men who are in search for established and credible advice for their fashion needs.

For Women

Channel Name: Arika Sato

Link: https://www.youtube.com/user/ArikaSato

Rank: 5

Description:

This is a more risqué channel for women who are flirtatious and not afraid to show off their bodies.

Statistics:

Total View Count: 18,724,971
Video Uploaded: 468
Number of Subscribers: 211,871
Average Likes vs. Dislike Ratio: 2,597 vs. 540 / 83% Liked
Average Frequency of Uploads: Once a week

Comments:
Content Progression & Value of Information
Aside from fashion and accessories, the channel also features the host's workouts, diets and product reviews.

Clarity of the Speaker's Voice and Content
The host lives the lifestyle that her channel promotes. Viewers cannot help but feel convinced to try the tips and tricks found on the videos.

Verdict: B

This is the perfect for channel for women who prefer the style and personality of the host. The channel shows more than fashion videos but the complete lifestyle.

Channel Name: La Madelynn

Link: https://www.youtube.com/user/LaMadelynn

Rank: 4

Description:

This channel offers a whimsical take on the world of fashion, it is relaxed and advices the natural look in beauty.

Statistics:

Total View Count: 2,614,715
Video Uploaded: 134
Number of Subscribers: 82,603
Average Likes vs. Dislike Ratio: 8,284 vs. 72 / 99% Liked
Average Frequency of Uploads: Once to twice a week

Comments:

Content Progression & Value of Information
The videos pair the suggested outfits with the season; this makes the channel very applicable and comprehensive the year round.

Clarity of the Speaker's Voice and Content
The host is sweet and very engaging, her opinions and preferences seem to reflect the same needs of her target demographic.

Verdict: B

For the female viewers who share the same style preference, this channel will offer the best set of information for fashion, accessories and more.

Channel Name: All Things Fabulous 101

Link: https://www.youtube.com/user/AllThingsFabulous101

Rank: 3

Description:

Complete with fashion, beauty, family and the entire gamut of women's lifestyle, this channel offers the more realistic side for fashion for more mature women.

Statistics:

Total View Count: 11,460,162
Video Uploaded: 335
Number of Subscribers: 197,610
Average Likes vs. Dislike Ratio: 5,325 vs. 127 / 98% Liked
Average Frequency of Uploads: Once to twice a week

Comments:

Content Progression & Value of Information
The videos including topics on fashion, beauty and other beauty needs make this channel the perfect companion for beginners.

Clarity of the Speaker's Voice and Content
The channel follows the life of host all the way to her current pregnancy status. This allows her to provide information on fashion advices for maternity dresses and other accessories.

Verdict: A

The 101 title says it all; this channel is for the woman, who wants to start with the fashionable lifestyle.

Channel Name: Dulce Candy

Link: https://www.youtube.com/user/DulceCandy87

Rank: 2

Description:

This channel offers fashion, beauty and hair tutorials for the modern woman; one of its unique offerings is to include her experience in plastic surgery.

Statistics:

Total View Count: 251,222,407
Video Uploaded: 762
Number of Subscribers: 1,920,303
Average Likes vs. Dislike Ratio: 3,931 vs. 1,380 / 74% Liked
Average Frequency of Uploads: Once a week

Comments:

Content Progression & Value of Information
Topics include beauty, hair and fashion tutorials, it covers one of the widest ranges of products and fashion finds.

Clarity of the Speaker's Voice and Content
The host is very engaging and makes smart use of camera focus and angles to emphasize her product reviews and messages.

Verdict: B

The sheer statistics alone make this channel a must watch for women viewers.

Channel Name: Vogue

Link: https://www.youtube.com/user/Americanvogue

Rank: 1

Description:

The eternal fashion bible, this channel is the virtual magazine for the highly respected publication.

Statistics:
Total View Count: 39,578,038
Video Uploaded: 1,304
Number of Subscribers: 236,080
Average Likes vs. Dislike Ratio: 10,375 vs. 200 / 98% Liked
Average Frequency of Uploads: Once to twice a week

Comments:

Content Progression & Value of Information
None can dispute the progeny of the information found in this channel. Under the guiding hands of the editor in chief, viewers can be sure of the credibility of the content.

Clarity of the Speaker's Voice and Content
The variety of hosts and guests in the channel complements the diverse topics covered in this channel.

Verdict: B

Despite the influence of the magazine and the brand, the statistics of the channel are relatively low compared to the other channels. This shows the paradox found in channels.

Chapter Eight: Makeup Tutorials

Channel Name: Andrea's Choice

Link: https://www.youtube.com/user/AndreasChoice

Rank: 5

Description:
Beauty hacks are the best selling videos of this channel. Aside from that it offers other tips on makeup and hairstyle.

Statistics:
Total View Count: 173,576,464
Video Uploaded: 186
Number of Subscribers: 3,136,180
Average Likes vs. Dislike Ratio: 9,828 vs. 3,952 / 71%
Average Frequency of Uploads: Once to twice a week

Comments:

Content Progression & Value of Information
DIY tips on makeup coupled with a flair for the cinematic make this an entertaining channel to watch.

Clarity of the Speaker's Voice and Content
The host is very chatty and high pitched, while this may be welcome to some viewers, it may also be disconcerting to others.

Verdict: C

A modern channel that makes use of the lifehack movement, easy and DIY tips and tricks for your makeup, fashion and even gifts ideas for the boyfriend, it is a must for the young and hip viewer out there.

Channel Name: Lisa Eldridge

Link: https://www.youtube.com/user/lisaeldridgedotcom

Rank: 4

Description:

The channel host is a professional makeup artist; she caters to celebrities, models and top brands in the market. Expertise on classic to barely there makeup make this channel and the videos a must see.

Statistics:

Total View Count: 82,909,020
Video Uploaded: 205
Number of Subscribers: 1,117,251
Average Likes vs. Dislike Ratio: 29,103 vs. 357 / 99% Liked
Average Frequency of Uploads: Once to twice a month

Comments:

Content Progression & Value of Information
Makeup topics range from old Hollywood to popular culture trends. The inspiration covers different makeup from different eras.

Clarity of the Speaker's Voice and Content
The host is very warm and engaging, she is a gentle speaker which makes viewers feel relaxed. This quality makes this channel very endearing because of the relative safety the channel can offer especially for conscious viewers.

Verdict: B

Aside from enhancing facial features, the host also gives make up techniques that can solve some usual problems, like covering scars, acne spots and wrinkles.

Channel Name: Cute Polish

Link: https://www.youtube.com/user/cutepolish

Rank: 3

Description:

A wholly dedicated channel for nail polish, these videos are carefully created and present several exciting ideas for this makeup for the hands and feet.

Statistics:

Total View Count: 287,022,829
Video Uploaded: 247
Number of Subscribers: 2,411,254
Average Likes vs. Dislike Ratio: 89,504 vs. 1,313 / 99% Liked
Average Frequency of Uploads: Once to twice a week

Comments:

Content Progression & Value of Information
Although very specific, the sheer creativity of this channel makes the videos truly valuable and may never be seen elsewhere.

Clarity of the Speaker's Voice and Content
The main attraction of this channel is the host, who is able to come up with a variety of designs and tips for this art.

Verdict: B

Instead of only solid colors, this channel elevates nail polish to the next level. Nail art provides tutorials on how to create pandas, Hello Kitty, newspaper, water marble, space art and a whole lot more.

Channel Name: Miss Glamorazzi

Link: https://www.youtube.com/user/missglamorazzi

Rank: 2

Description:

Beauty, fashion, healthy food and several DIY projects make this channel about makeup all the more appealing.

Statistics:

Total View Count: 242,595,112
Video Uploaded: 454
Number of Subscribers: 3,268,978
Average Likes vs. Dislike Ratio: 45,105 vs. 834 / 98% Liked
Average Frequency of Uploads: Once to twice a week

Comments:

Content Progression & Value of Information
The favorite videos make the channel easy to navigate, this way casual viewers will be able to take on the gist of the channel and explore others when interested.

Clarity of the Speaker's Voice and Content
The host is friendly and speaks in a clear and audible tone. She knows exactly what she is talking about and is more than confident to share her ideas with her viewers.

Verdict: B

This total beauty channel includes makeup, hairstyle, fashion, skincare and a monthly collection of favorite items. This is a promising channel with great potential.

Channel Name: Michelle Phan

Link: https://www.youtube.com/user/MichellePhan

Rank: 1

Description:

A channel that has ignited the success of the host, it has videos dedicated to makeup and the entire beauty lifestyle.

Statistics:

Total View Count: 1,097,312,738
Video Uploaded: 357
Number of Subscribers: 7,593,450
Average Likes vs. Dislike Ratio: 120,022 vs. 16,840 / 88% Liked
Average Frequency of Uploads: Once to twice a week

Comments:

Content Progression & Value of Information
The videos are engaging and very practical both for beginner and expert makeup artists.

Clarity of the Speaker's Voice and Content
A very friendly and humble host that is already an expert in the makeup industry, she gives authenticity to the concept of being able to do the makeup on the viewer's own.

Verdict: A

The channel represents the potential for channel owner to make a lucrative business and reputation for themselves. The staggering statistics of the channel catapulted the owner to media channels outside Youtube.

Chapter Nine: Parenting Advice & Stories

Channel Name: Umbumgo

Link: https://www.youtube.com/user/umbumgo

Rank: 5

Description:

This is a long running channel that covers the parenting life of the host starting from the pregnancy for her first son and now with 5 children.

Statistics:

Total View Count: 8,859,777
Video Uploaded: 702
Number of Subscribers: 12,407
Average Likes vs. Dislike Ratio: 434 vs. 163 / 73% Liked
Average Frequency of Uploads: Twice to thrice a week

Comments:

Content Progression & Value of Information
This channel covers the daily life and challenges of a mom, from raising her children, to doing the groceries and other household chores.

Clarity of the Speaker's Voice and Content
The host speaks from experience and usually shows her tips being applied throughout her videos, along with her partner and children.

Verdict: B

Nothing gives more credibility than experiencing the topics; this channel is able to provide sound advice that may not come from an actual parenting expert but from a parent herself.

Channel Name: The Scheurman Show

Link: https://www.youtube.com/user/theschuermanshow

Rank: 4

Description:

This channel follows the lives of the Scheurman family. It has a video for every member of the family, from the father, mother and the kids. It covers about the host finding out that she is pregnant all the way to raising the children.

Statistics:

Total View Count: 12,038,288
Video Uploaded: 868
Number of Subscribers: 69,111
Average Likes vs. Dislike Ratio: 890 vs. 76 / 92% Liked
Average Frequency of Uploads: Once a day

Comments:

Content Progression & Value of Information
Videos are more of a recording of the daily lives of the family members. While the content may not provide expert parenting advice, the reality of the family life is shared to viewers.

Clarity of the Speaker's Voice and Content
While most parenting channel features only the mother of the family, getting the perspective of all members of the family, like the husband, gives another dimension to this channel.

Verdict: C

This channel is able to ground viewers to the reality of parenting and family life. Instead of a clinical perspective of the issue, it shows a practical and extremely realistic viewpoint.

Channel Name: Katie & Baby

Link: https://www.youtube.com/user/81KatieMarie

Rank: 3

Description:

This is channel for raising infants. It covers everything from making baby foods to safety concerns. Newborn must haves are also added.

Statistics:

Total View Count: 2,431,665
Video Uploaded: 302
Number of Subscribers: 17,692
Average Likes vs. Dislike Ratio: 900 vs. 106 / 89% Liked
Average Frequency of Uploads: Once to twice a week

Comments:

Content Progression & Value of Information
The videos cover everything needed prior, during and the few months after childbirth.

Clarity of the Speaker's Voice and Content
The host may be young but her first hand experience of the topics involved gives her credibility.

Verdict: A

The practicality and the focus of this channel give it top marks. This channel is valuable especially for first time mothers or parents.

Channel Name: My Smart Hands

Link: https://www.youtube.com/user/SmartHandsCA

Rank: 2

Description:

Videos about children friendly recipes, crafts and parenting advice are included in this channel.

Statistics:

Total View Count: 29,107,744
Video Uploaded: 569
Number of Subscribers: 29,364
Average Likes vs. Dislike Ratio: 4,852 vs. 651 / 88% Liked
Average Frequency of Uploads: Once a week

Comments:

Content Progression & Value of Information
One of the highlights is the videos on traveling with the family. There are also videos on how parents can educate their children.

Clarity of the Speaker's Voice and Content
The host translates her creativity not only on crafts but also on parenting. She combines the two to make engaging parenting tips and tricks.

Verdict: B

Instead of placing the burden on the mother alone, the essence of the channel is parenting through family activities.

Channel Name: Kids in the House

Link: https://www.youtube.com/user/kidsinthehouseTV

Rank: 1

Description:

This channel provides parenting tips and advice to parents. Videos are from the combined efforts of experts, professionals and parents.

Statistics:

Total View Count: 1,141,613
Video Uploaded: 967
Number of Subscribers: 2,448
Average Likes vs. Dislike Ratio: 963 vs. 10 / 99%
Average Frequency of Uploads: Once to twice a week

Comments:

Content Progression & Value of Information
The videos cover one of the most comprehensive ranges of topics in the category. It gives advice for parents of infants all the way to teenage life. Current issues such as a bullying and self-esteem issues are covered.

Clarity of the Speaker's Voice and Content
The power of this channel comes from the expert content provided by the professionals and parents who lend their experience and knowledge to the viewers.

Verdict: A

The depth of the videos in the channel coming from a pool of resource persons allows for the top ratings.

Chapter Ten: Dating & Relationships

Channel Name: Simple Pickup

Link: https://www.youtube.com/user/SimplePickup

Rank: 5

Description:

This is channel that attempts to prove that any man can date and attract women. They use pickup lines and interviews with the opposite sex to gain tips.

Statistics:

Total View Count: 261,192,239
Video Uploaded: 157
Number of Subscribers: 2,152,278
Average Likes vs. Dislike Ratio: 55,779 vs. 5,606 / 91% Liked
Average Frequency of Uploads: Once a week

Comments:

Content Progression & Value of Information
The videos objectify women with their topics and videos. Viewers, who do not share the host's opinions, may be offended.

Clarity of the Speaker's Voice and Content
The two hosts are unapologetic in their videos. They know exactly the emptiness but effectiveness of their tips.

Verdict: B

The statistics alone makes up for the lack of depth of this channel. This shows that content does not always have to be mainstream to be successful.

Channel Name: Matthew J. Dempsey

Link: https://www.youtube.com/user/matthewjdempsey

Rank: 4

Description:

This is a channel that focuses on the life and relationship advice especially for the gay male community.

Statistics:

Total View Count: 334,621
Video Uploaded: 11
Number of Subscribers: 5,341
Average Likes vs. Dislike Ratio: 417 vs. 14 / 97% Liked
Average Frequency of Uploads: Once a month

Comments:

Content Progression & Value of Information
The videos cover topics such as attraction, breaking up, keeping love alive and judgment.

Clarity of the Speaker's Voice and Content
The host speaks in a clear voice; he is able to put into perspective modern issues using sound advice based on psychology.

Verdict: A

This channel provides good information in a niche category, which may be rare in this category.

Channel Name: Worth the Wait

Link:
https://www.youtube.com/user/WorthTheWait518/featured

Rank: 3

Description:

This channel offers relationship advice using a Christian's perspective.

Statistics:

Total View Count: 103,203
Video Uploaded: 23
Number of Subscribers: 3,550
Average Likes vs. Dislike Ratio: 446vs. 4 / 99% Liked
Average Frequency of Uploads: Once to twice a week

Comments:
Content Progression & Value of Information
This channel documents the courtship and engagement of a couple, who puts God in the center of their relationship. It offers advice for those dating, ready to date and in a relationship.

Clarity of the Speaker's Voice and Content
The hosts, who are also real life couples, give credibility to their topics for viewers who share the same faith.

Verdict: A

Despite the low statistics, this channel offers a rare insight on a usually overlooked perspective on relationship.

Channel Name: Practical Happiness

Link: https://www.youtube.com/user/arkady39

Rank: 2

Description:

This channel offers tips and advice not only on relationships but also on dating.

Statistics:

Total View Count: 10,932,368
Video Uploaded: 264
Number of Subscribers: 18,484
Average Likes vs. Dislike Ratio: 2,120 vs. 98 / 96% Liked
Average Frequency of Uploads: Once a month

Comments:

Content Progression & Value of Information
This channel offers clear and concrete advice for both men and women from first dates, to break ups, to rejection and other relationship issues.

Clarity of the Speaker's Voice and Content
The host is very engaging. He makes use of clear examples with demonstrations. He regularly bases his topics on requests from his viewers.

Verdict: B

The value of this channel is that it translates the concepts it shares with practical and actionable steps that viewers can immediately apply after watching.

Channel Name: Dating With Dignity

Link: https://www.youtube.com/user/datingwithdignity

Rank: 1

Description:

This channel provides tools, lines and practical tips for finding and keeping love.

Statistics:

Total View Count: 4,265,286
Video Uploaded: 108
Number of Subscribers: 20,084
Average Likes vs. Dislike Ratio: 1,471 vs. 169 / 90% Liked
Average Frequency of Uploads: Once a week

Comments:

Content Progression & Value of Information
This channel covers a wide variety of dating and romance topics that deal with first dates, breakup and other relationship advice in between.

Clarity of the Speaker's Voice and Content
The host is a relationship and dating coach, who regularly conducts seminars and talks. She is able to invite guests, who share their own unique perspective in the category.

Verdict: A

Due to the guests and resource person that the host invites, viewers are able to gain advice not only from the host's own perspective but also from her guests and listeners.

Chapter Eleven: Motivation & Inspiration

Channel Name: The Journey of Purpose

Link: https://www.youtube.com/user/TheJourneyofPurpose

Rank: 5

Description:

A channel that offers videos for wonder, passion and purpose, it has stunning scenes that complement the narration.

Statistics:

Total View Count: 6,161,220
Video Uploaded: 30
Number of Subscribers: 89,771
Average Likes vs. Dislike Ratio: 8,034 vs. 94 / 99% Liked
Average Frequency of Uploads: Once a week

Comments:

Content Progression & Value of Information
The channel includes topics on self-identity, following your heart and finding purpose and meaning in life.

Clarity of the Speaker's Voice and Content
The makers of the video collect a variety of inspirational quotes and sound bites from well-known individuals.

Verdict: B

The channel is thought provoking; the voice of the narrator gives a soothing yet firm take on his message.

Channel Name: Peak Your Mind

Link: https://www.youtube.com/user/PeakYourMind

Rank: 4

Description:

This channel is about self-improvement, social skills and psychology. The host is young and hip but serious and mature.

Statistics:

Total View Count: 893,729
Video Uploaded: 59
Number of Subscribers: 21,958
Average Likes vs. Dislike Ratio: 2,245 vs. 51 / 98% Liked
Average Frequency of Uploads: Twice a week

Comments:

Content Progression & Value of Information
The videos cover a wide range of topics that can be well-received by viewers who have different kinds of motivational issues.

Clarity of the Speaker's Voice and Content
The host is open to his viewer's comments and inquiry, his positivity is apparent in his way of speaking.

Verdict: A

A unique channel that dispels the stereotype of old and wise motivational coaches, the young host makes him relatable to an equally young demographic.

Channel Name: Yayha Bakkar

Link: https://www.youtube.com/user/YahyaBakkar

Rank: 3

Description:

The philosophy of this channel is that for true change to occur, you must take care of yourself from the inside out.

Statistics:

Total View Count: 549,574
Video Uploaded: 68
Number of Subscribers: 10,509
Average Likes vs. Dislike Ratio: 259 vs. 6 / 98% Liked
Average Frequency of Uploads: Once every two weeks

Comments:
Content Progression & Value of Information
Purpose, perfection, communication, forgiveness and other life issues are discussed in this video.

Clarity of the Speaker's Voice and Content
The host combines the physical with the psychological element of motivation to resolve issues such as confidence, depression, anxiety, courage and clarity.

Verdict: A

The format of the videos is very refreshing. Instead of abstract ideas, the host makes use of a how-to guide to enable readers to have clear steps on what to do after watching the videos.

Channel Name: Mateusz M

Link: https://www.youtube.com/user/TheMir00r/featured

Rank: 2

Description:

A selection of videos compiled from clips and originals, the visuals and sounds bites are stunning even in their minimalistic theme.

Statistics:

Total View Count: 81,299,408
Video Uploaded: 19
Number of Subscribers: 446,246
Average Likes vs. Dislike Ratio: 207,620 vs. 3,639 / 98% Liked
Average Frequency of Uploads: Once a month

Comments:
Content Progression & Value of Information
The topics are very enticing; the makers use one word or short phrases that can entice viewers.

Clarity of the Speaker's Voice and Content
The creativity of the makers of this channel is expressed when they weave together a variety of clips coupled with sound bites taken from a variety of sources. The background music complements the messages.

Verdict: A

One of the channels with the smallest number of videos but with one of the greatest numbers of views and subscribers, this channel relies on quality over quantity.

Channel Name: Good Life Project

Link: https://www.youtube.com/user/CareerRenegade

Rank: 1

Description:

This is a channel that shows interviews with weekly guests from all backgrounds, such as entrepreneurs, artists, and leaders of the industry. The main goal is to explore what it means to have a good life.

Statistics:

Total View Count: 3,166,590
Video Uploaded: 170
Number of Subscribers: 37,160
Average Likes vs. Dislike Ratio: 7,728 vs. 304 / 96% Liked
Average Frequency of Uploads: Once a month

Comments:

Content Progression & Value of Information
The host regularly invites guests to his channel to talk about a wide range of motivational topics, such as vulnerability, habit, excellence, passion, failure, judgment and other topics.

Clarity of the Speaker's Voice and Content
The host, a motivational speaker, offers advice coming from experience. His personal stories are the inspiration to most of the videos where he himself is the resource person.

Verdict: A

This is a channel that draws its content from the guests, who act as resource persons and motivational speakers in their respective videos. This gives viewers access to not only the perspective of the host but also to the hundreds of guest in the channel.

Conclusion

The channels included in the Manifesto represent only the tip of the iceberg. For sure, as new videos are uploaded, new channels are made. With new channels, come more views, more likes and more subscribers. This shows that in Youtube, the possibilities are endless and the only limit is that of the host's knowledge, creativity and passion for the chosen category.

A successful Youtube channel does not rely on high production budgets, popular culture or expert knowledge. Even with just a webcam, a niche topic and passion for the content, a channel can potentially satisfy your curiosity and need for information. Remember, do not judge a channel by their statistics alone, you need to read between the lines or in this case, the video clips. See beyond numbers, look at the hosts, listen to the content and discern between simple popularity and actual legitimacy.

I hope that this book was able to point you out to some of the best channels in Youtube. The important lesson in this book is not to choose among the channels listed but to learn to have the solid foundation on how to find, choose and ultimately how to learn from the channels.

Happy watching!

www.ingramcontent.com/pod-product-compliance
Lightning Source LLC
Chambersburg PA
CBHW070836180526

45168CB00002B/849